MASTER YOUR ENGLISH

Verbs

G. C. Davies, L.C.P.
S. M. Dillon
C. Egerton-Chesney
Illustrated by G. C. Davies

SIMON & SCHUSTER
EDUCATION

To children using this book

This book is intended to increase your knowledge of verbs and their correct use.

You can practise your knowledge of verbs in many ways — one way would be to use some of the characters in this book in stories or other writing. You could, for example, write some more film scripts for Hiram Z. Bigglezetter to direct, or you could invent some more adventures for the soldiers of King Munch's Army.

To teachers using this book

It is not essential to use this book sequentially throughout, particularly if the children already possess some knowledge of the topics in this book. Most teachers, however, will prefer to deal with the simpler concepts at the beginning of the book before proceeding to the more advanced work. The Munchtest on pages 31 and 32 may be used for diagnostic purposes or for revision.

© 1981 G. C. Davies, S. M. Dillon and C. Egerton-Chesney

First published in 1981 by
Basil Blackwell Ltd
Reprinted 1982, 1985, 1989

Reprinted in 1992, 1993 by
Simon and Schuster Education

Simon and Schuster Education
Campus 400
Maylands Avenue
Hemel Hempstead
Herts HP2 7EZ

All rights reserved. No part of this publication may be reproduced, stored in a retrieval system, or transmitted, in any form or by any means, electronic, mechanical, recording or otherwise, without the prior permission of Simon and Schuster Education.

ISBN 0 7501 0384 1

Printed in Great Britain by T. J. Press (Padstow) Ltd.

CONTENTS

		Page
1	What is a verb?	4
2	Finding verbs	6
3	'Activity' verbs	7
4	'Sound' verbs	8
5	Choosing verbs	9
6	Fast, slow, quiet and loud verbs	10
7	Actions	11
8	Making sentences	12
9	Past and present tense	13
10	Changing from one tense to another	15
11	Future tense	21
12	How many words in a verb?	24
13	Using verbs as adjectives	26
14	Using verbs as nouns	28
15	Using nouns as verbs	30
	Munchtest	31/32

1. What is a verb?

How not to ride a bicycle
A short film starring Mandy Smith

This is the story-line of a film script to be directed by the Hollywood director, Hiram Z. Bigglezetter.

The great day dawned when Sally Gibb could try out her new Superzoom bicycle.

She leapt on to the saddle and shot down the front path just in time to crash into the milk float that arrived outside the gate at that moment. The milkman was very angry and shouted that her father would have to pay for the dent in the float and for the broken bottles.

Not that Sally cared. She giggled with excitement as she shot off again, only to collide with a lamp-post.

Still Sally continued her destructive progress. She ripped her new jeans, flattened the tail of next-door's cat, knocked the postman into the gutter, ran over P.C. Jordan's feet and crashed into a pillar-box, ending up draped over it. Her cycling adventures ended there.

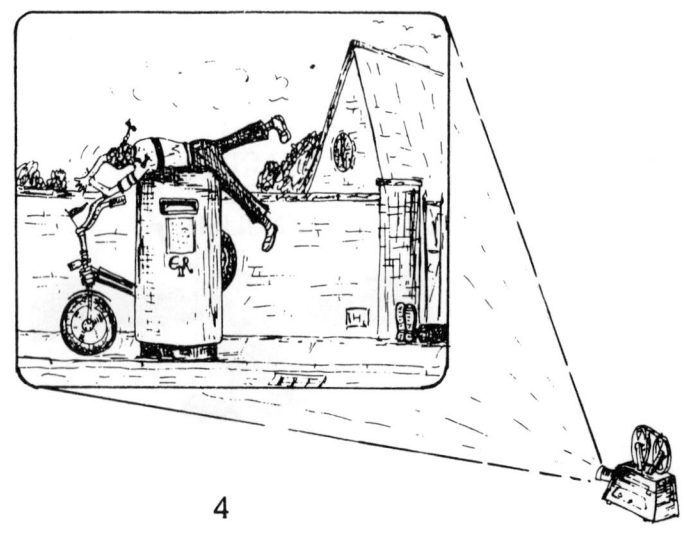

Hiram Z. Bigglezetter gave his directions . . . .

"*Leap* on the saddle of the bicycle. Now *ride* down the front path. Charlie, you *arrive* at the gate at the same time. Camera, *zoom* in on Sally's face . . ."

The words in *italics* are 'action words' or 'doing words'. The proper name for such words is a **verb**.

Write down the verbs in these five sentences.

1. She giggled with excitement.
2. Sally continued her destructive progress.
3. She ripped her new jeans.
4. The great day dawned.
5. The bicycle crashed into the milk float.

> Find five more verbs in the 'story-line' on page 4, then write them down in sentences of your own.

2. Finding verbs

A Find the verbs in these sentences. Each sentence has one verb.

1. Tie your shoelaces tightly.
2. Give me those sweets at once.
3. Pick up that load carefully.
4. The fire crackled noisily.
5. Jack fell down this morning.

B Now find the two verbs in each of the sentences below.

1. Father grumbled because Sally broke her bicycle.
2. Chew slowly and eat carefully.
3. Fry the eggs and boil the potatoes.
4. Sam broke his arm and fractured his leg.
5. First catch the fish then freeze it.
6. The dog sat quietly for a while and then it barked noisily.
7. John stood up and hobbled slowly to the open door.
8. Mary ran after the bus and, very stupidly, she jumped on.

3. 'Action' verbs

A Complete these sentences by putting in suitable verbs.

1. _____ the dart into the bullseye.
2. I like to _____ letters on my typewriter.
3. How long can you _____ on one leg?
4. I will go and _____ some bacon and eggs.
5. Climb to the top and _____ all the way down.
6. You are so dirty that you must _____ your face.

B Write down the verbs that say in one word what action is being done in these phrases.

Examples: To shake with cold – the verb is *shiver*
     To heat water until it bubbles – the verb is *boil*

1. To disappear completely
2. To put on one's clothes
3. To take off one's clothes
4. To make a hole in something with a tool
5. To hit someone with a closed fist
6. To jump into water, hands first
7. To breathe in and out very quickly
8. To move forward, putting one foot in front of the other
9. To produce a picture using brush and paints
10. To chew and swallow food

4. 'Sound' verbs

A Match the 'sound' verbs below to the animals that make them.

Animals	Sounds
1. a turkey	mews
2. a bee	neighs
3. a pigeon	gobbles
4. a horse	grunts
5. a cow	hums
6. a donkey	lows
7. a cat	coos
8. a pig	brays

B Match these 'sound' verbs to the things that make them.

Things	Sounds
1. a whip	rolls
2. a bell	patters
3. a siren	cracks
4. a drum	rustle
5. paper	crackles
6. thunder	rings
7. leaves	bangs
8. rain	wails

5. Choosing verbs

Choose verbs to fit into these sentences. Your sentences must make sense.

1. Private Pop was told to _____ up the flag.
2. Sergeant Snap _____ very loudly.
3. Captain Crackle _____ a white horse.
4. General Crunch _____ lemonade when he is thirsty.
5. Corporal Gobble _____ the Army's tank.
6. King Munch _____ over Munchland.
7. Private Chew likes to _____ his buttons.
8. Private Bonehead _____ the Army's porridge.
9. The Munchland Army has never _____ a war.
10. King Munch's soldiers _____ his castle.
11. The soldiers have to _____ up and down all day.
12. Each soldier _____ a wooden rifle on his shoulder.

6. Fast, slow, quiet and loud

Write down these 'movement' verbs in two lists, fast movements and slow movements

run   creep
dart   charge
hurry   dawdle
hurtle amble
meander crawl

whisper   rustle   bang   roar

hiss   bellow

thunder   patter

shout   purr

scream   screech

tinkle   swish

tick   howl

yelp   yell

sob   mutter   snarl   twitter

Put these 'sound' verbs into two lists, quiet verbs and loud verbs

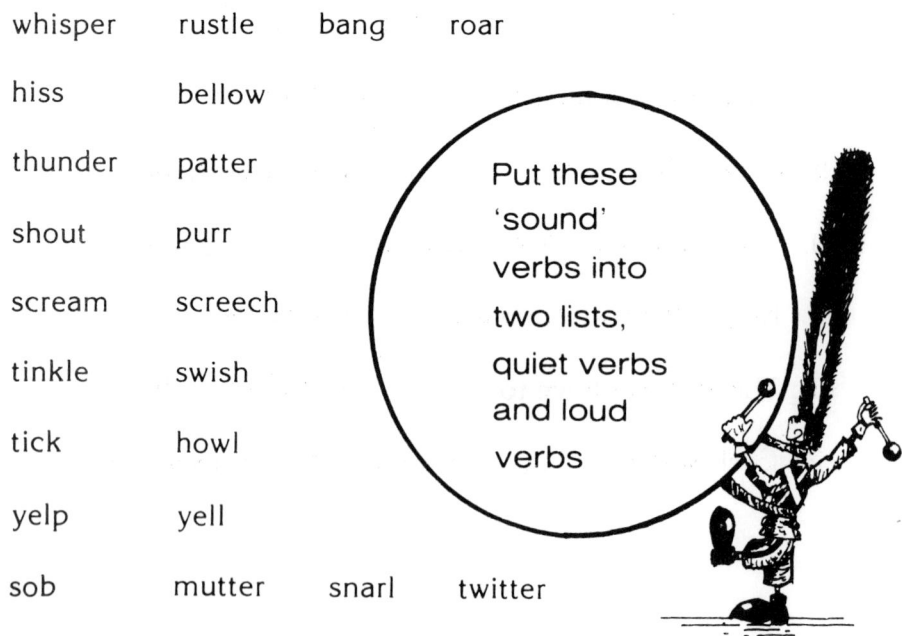

7. Actions

Private Gulp is the Munchland Army's gardener. These are some of his actions in the Royal Gardens.

> He *digs*
>
> *rakes   mows   weeds*
>
> *plants   hoes*

Write down two more verbs for each of these actions.
Like this:
    papering a room   :   *measuring....cutting, pasting*

1. playing football   :   kicking .....
2. playing netball   :   running.....
3. cleaning a house   :   dusting.....
4. baking a cake   :   stirring.....
5. making a picture   :   drawing.....
6. making a model   :   cutting, glueing.....
7. riding a bicycle   :   balancing, steering.....
8. fishing   :   baiting, casting.....
9. flying a kite   :   running, pulling.....
10. riding on a bus   :   boarding, paying.....

8. Making sentences

Dream up eight sentences using one or more of these verbs in each sentence. Use each verb once only.

teach	know	
swim	catch	
eat	fight	beat
mow	run	shout
ring	fall	televise
write	kneel	direct
throw	drink	chase
lay	creep	explain
act	advertise	resist
fly	travel	flop
crow	print	jeer
kill	drop	hate

9. Past and present tense

King Munch's new helicopter

Corporal Gobble had learnt how to fly King Munch's new helicopter. He flew the machine over the parade ground as the whole Army watched. The soldiers stood, stared and chattered. What excitement!

"Did you see?" squeaked Private Pop, "The helicopter flied round the castle tower!"

Private Chew squealed, "And it flewed backwards!"

"And it flowded sideways!" chattered Private Gulp.

"Then it fleeded up and down!" gabbled Private Bonehead.

Sergeant Snap, who had just come along, bellowed, "Flewed, flied, flowded, fleeded! You silly privates. The helicopter *flew*!"

Of course, Sergeant Snap was right.

The helicopter flies *now* . . . in the *present*

The helicopter flew *then* . . . in the *past*

ten minutes ago   last month   last year   yesterday
are all in the *past*

flew is the past **tense** of flies

flies is the present **tense**

tense means *time*

> Verbs in the past tense describe actions that have already taken place.

present tense	past tense
Sam walks	Sam walked
Edward cries	Edward cried
Mary runs	Mary ran
Snap shouts	Snap shouted
Mum laughs	Mum laughed
Jason prays	Jason prayed
Tom hops	Tom hopped

10. Changing from one tense to another

When a sentence changes from one tense to another the verb often changes.

Examples

present tense	past tense
I love	I loved
it lives	it lived
you mend	you mended
I pat	I patted
we try	we tried

Some verbs do not change.... Examples:

present tense	past tense
I cut the bread now	I cut the bread yesterday
Now we put the baby into the cot	We put the baby into the cot last night

Here are ways in which you change verbs when a sentence changes from the present tense to the past tense.

> 1. You put **ed** on the end of the verb (and drop the **s**).

Examples: I walk ... I *walked*
Mary laughs ... Mary *laughed*
Sam pulls ... Sam *pulled*

Rewrite these sentences in the past tense

1. Mary screams suddenly.
2. I kick the ball.
3. The frog jumps on to the lily.
4. The spider kills the fly.
5. I long for my home.
6. Many people like to listen to local radio.

15

> 2. Some verbs that end in **es** change the **s** to **d**.

Examples:

General Crunch decides — General Crunch *decided*

King Munch waves — King Munch *waved*

> **A** Change these sentences from the present tense to the past tense.

1. Tom wastes his money.
2. Sergeant Snap scares the soldiers.
3. Nobody notices little me.
4. The chef prepares his own sauce.
5. The king settles the argument.

> **B** Change these sentences from the past tense to the present tense.

1. Everyone admired the view.
2. Tarzan explored the dark cave.
3. The train arrived on time.
4. Aunt Maud asked about the price of the blue suitcase.
5. The referee declared Jones the winner of the boxing-match.

> 3. Some verbs change one or more letters.

Examples:

I draw a picture — I *drew* a picture

Linda runs quickly — Linda *ran* quickly

Private Pop falls over — Private Pop *fell* over

Kate weeps bitterly — Kate *wept* bitterly

> **A** Change these sentences from the present tense to the past tense.

1. Mrs. Davies teaches me cookery.
2. The pond freezes every winter.
3. The rocket rises into the sky.
4. Hitler speaks to a huge crowd.
5. Kim draws a beautiful picture.

> **B** Change these sentences from the past tense to the present tense.

1. Richard rose very early.
2. William sat on the wall.
3. Naughty Thomas broke all his toys.
4. Hector ate all his cake.
5. Simon kept his models in his room.

> 4. Some verbs that end in **y** change the *y* to **ied**.

> 5. Some verbs that end in **ies** change the *s* to **d**.

Examples:
  Cooks fry eggs — Cooks *fried* eggs
  Athletes try hard — Athletes *tried* hard
  Your baby cries loudly — Your baby *cried* loudly
  Tim qualifies for a prize — Tim *qualified* for a prize

Change these sentences from the present tense to the past tense.

1. Some babies cry all night.
2. A good boy tries hard to be first.
3. Strong men carry heavy loads.
4. The secret agent spies on everyone.
5. Robert's mother worries about him.
6. Most prisoners deny the charges.
7. That big black dog terrifies me.
8. Simon always lies instead of being truthful.

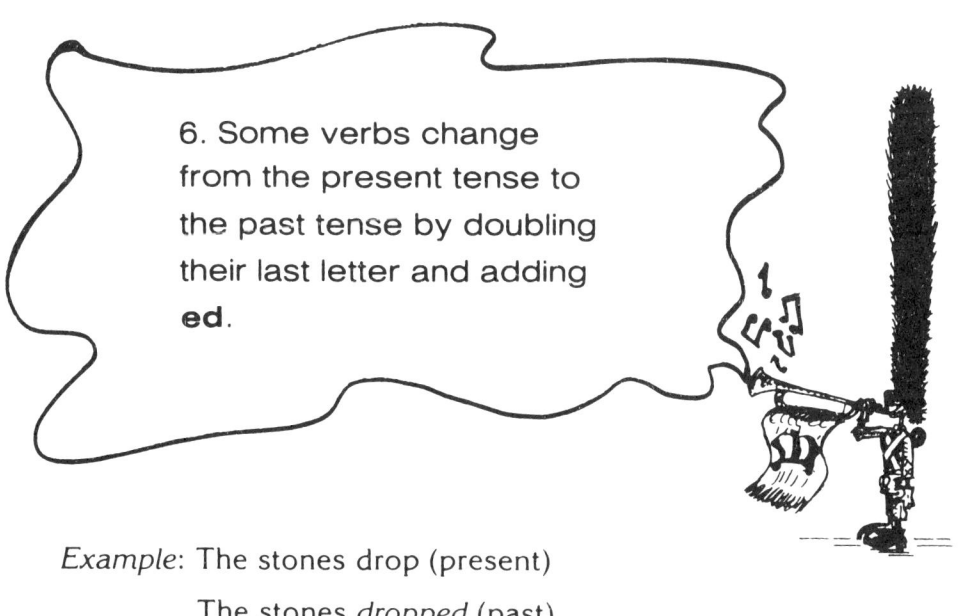

6. Some verbs change from the present tense to the past tense by doubling their last letter and adding **ed**.

Example: The stones drop (present)
 The stones *dropped* (past)

Change these sentences from the present tense to the past tense.

1. The soldiers scrub the floor.
2. Ten flags flap in the street.
3. Elizabeth mops the floor.
4. Joe, the cheeky chimp, claps loudly.
5. The waiter pops the cork.
6. My old aunt shops very carefully.
7. The broken branch of the tree sags dangerously.
8. Aunt Maud hugs little Teddy every time she sees him.*

* *Think! There are two verbs in this sentence.*

Correct these sentences.

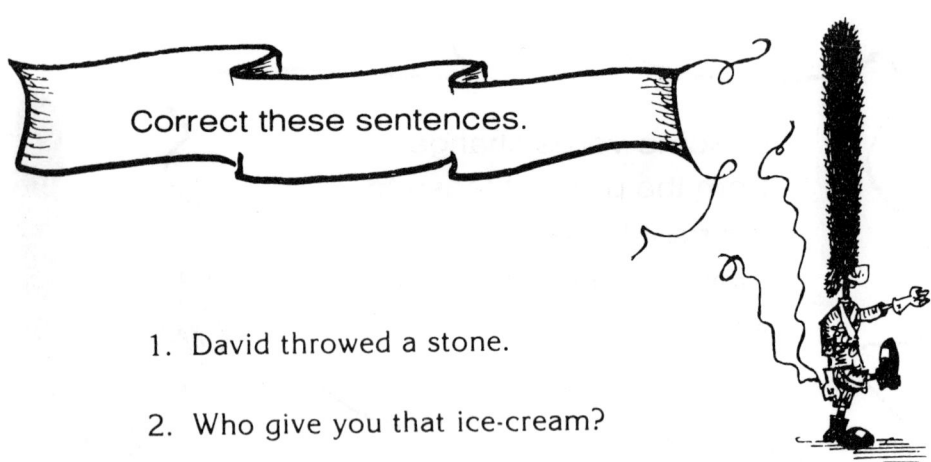

1. David throwed a stone.
2. Who give you that ice-cream?
3. The choir sung three songs.
4. Wendy catched a cold last week.
5. We drunk our milk slowly.
6. The helicopter flowed overhead.
7. Joe drawed that picture.
8. I writed the letter twice.
9. We eated our supper quickly.
10. I know who done the damage.
11. Eddie runned all the way home.
12. Dad nearly freezed to death.

11. Future tense

Private Bonehead was marching away from his sentry-box. Sergeant Snap bellowed at him.

"Where are you going, Private?" he bawled.

Bonehead stopped. "For a cup of tea, Sergeant," he quavered.

Snap's moustache wobbled and whiffled. He barked, "You stay and *guard* the castle, my lad."

Bonehead looked very hurt. "But I *guarded* it yesterday," he said.

Snap snorted impatiently and snarled, "And you *will guard* it again tomorrow!"

"Why, Sergeant?" asked poor old Bonehead.

The sergeant's face turned purple and he bellowed, "In case someone tries to steal it, of course!"

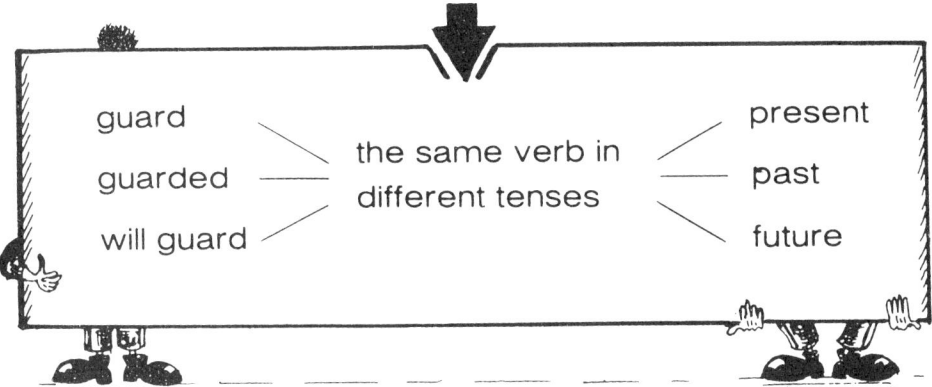

guard — the same verb in different tenses — present
guarded — past
will guard — future

A Change these sentences from the present tense to the future tense.

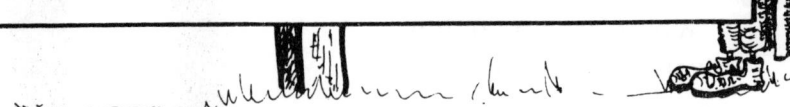

1. The ghost walks at midnight.

2. Sergeant Snap shouts at everybody.

3. Kim and Tim visit the dentist.

4. The fair comes on Bank Holidays.

5. The egg hatches into a baby dragon.

B Change these sentences from the past tense to the future tense.

1. The vandals smashed the playground.

2. Mr. Green sold six units.

3. Jemima screamed non-stop.

4. Chris laughed at the film with Laurel and Hardy in it.

5. Tek, the fat space-boy visited the planet Inviz yesterday. (*Think about this one!*)

6. Porky ate too much, as usual.

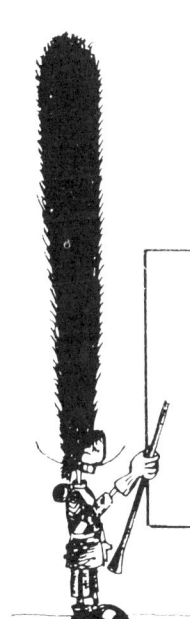

Sergeant Snap's Tense-test

Now pay attention! Change these sentences from the past tense to the present tense. After you have done this, write them out in the future tense.

1. Joseph kept the shoes.
2. King Munch gave General Crunch a lecture.
3. The alarm clock stopped at midnight.
4. The pump gave a cough and no more petrol came out.
5. Private Bonehead's helmet fell over his eyes and he collided with the sergeant.
6. Mum burnt the apple pie and she was furious.
7. Private Pop was late on parade so Corporal Gobble told him off.
8. The film began with a cowboy riding across the plain in a thunderstorm.
9. Old MacDonald had a farm and all his animals were sick.
10. The turkey heard Farmer White talking about Christmas and dropped dead with fright.

12. How many words in a verb?

Private Puff is the Munchland trumpeter.

If we think about what he does, we can say this about him blowing his trumpet:

Private Puff *blows* his trumpet

Private Puff *is blowing* his trumpet

Private Puff *was blowing* his trumpet

Private Puff *has blown* his trumpet

Private Puff *has been blowing* his trumpet

Private Puff *will have been blowing* his trumpet

Private Puff *will be blowing* his trumpet

By this time, of course, he will be out of breath!

All the words in italic print are the *verbs* of the sentences. You can see that most of the verbs are written with *more than one word*.

We are only going to think about verbs of *two* words.

Here are some more examples:

Private Gnash *is banging* a drum

Private Gnash *was banging* a drum

King Munch *is sitting* on his throne

King Munch *was sitting* on his throne

Private Pop *is marching* up and down

Private Pop *was marching* up and down

All the words in *italics* are verbs, and they are verbs with *two* words.

Like this:
> The rocket *falls* like a stone
> The rocket *is falling* like a stone
>
>   or
>
> The rocket *has fallen* like a stone
>
>   or
>
> The rocket *was falling* like a stone

As you can see, you can use verbs in the present tense *or* the past tense.

1. I *climb* the mountain today.

2. Those flowers *grow* very tall.

3. The birds *sing* sweetly.

4. The bull *chases* Terry.

5. The parachutist *falls* too quickly.

6. Private Puff *plays* the flute.

7. Dean *cleaned* his shoes.

8. Tracey *brushed* her teeth.

9. Captain Crackle *looks* after the Army's clock.

10. Policemen *spoke* to all the neighbours.

11. The Queen *stays* in bed.

12. Her dog *barks* at Sergeant Snap.

13. Using verbs as adjectives

The verbs in the sentences below have two words in them.

The second word of the verb, in *italics*, can also be used as an adjective.

We call such words *participles*.

> Private Pop is *marching* along.
>
> Uncle is *walking* in the rain.
>
> We were *singing* a happy tune.

This is how they can be used:

> What a splendid *marching* band.
>
> I had a *walking* doll for Christmas.
>
> Listen to that toy *singing* bird.

Here are some more examples:

Participles used as adjectives

> The tanks were *creeping* forward.   a *creeping* beetle
>
> Leaves are *falling* early.   the *falling* tree
>
> Frogs are *jumping* everywhere.   *jumping* beans

1. Harry was whistling a pop song.
2. Jet aircraft are flying all night.
3. The north wind is howling.
4. Sirens are warning the people to take shelter.
5. Poor Sarah is crying bitterly.
6. Boats were speeding across the bay.

Invent new sentences, using the participles from these sentences as adjectives

The words in *italics* in the sentences below are also participles and can be used as adjectives.

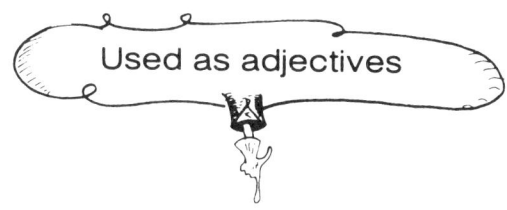
Used as adjectives

The window was *broken*.   a *broken* doll

Rovers have *beaten* United.   a *beaten* army

Ellen has *knitted* some gloves. a *knitted* sweater

Unlike the participles on page 26, they do not end in *ing*.

They can end in **d**   a dead body

         n   a torn dress

         t   a lost ball

         ed   a pointed stick

         en   stolen jewels

Invent new sentences, to include the participles from these sentences used as adjectives.

1. The treasure was hidden in the oak tree.
2. Martin has torn his trousers.
3. The warrior battered at the door.
4. Simon has filled the bucket with mud.
5. The pilot spotted fighters in the distance.
6. Jeremy has bent the wheel of his bicycle.

14. Using verbs as nouns

In these sentences the participles can be used as *nouns*. All the participles end in *ing*.

Verbs can be used as nouns.

The tramp was *walking* slowly. I enjoy *walking*.

Emily is *knitting* some socks. *Knitting* is a pleasant hobby.

Gliding is great fun.

Dream up sentences using nouns made from these verbs.

1. shout
2. smile
3. shine
4. fight
5. sink
6. fight
7. drink
8. whisper
9. wish
10. cry

More practice

Find the verbs in these sentences and use the participles as nouns in new sentences.

Reminder

The pilot was *praying* for a soft landing.
Praying should be done on one's knees.
Oscar is *washing* his socks.
Dirty *washing* should be put in the bin.

1. Tom is giving sweets to his friends.
2. Uncle Arthur was painting a picture.
3. Mum is patching my jacket.
4. The builders were measuring the wall.
5. Mr Beak is marking Wilfred's book.
6. Old Dobbin was jogging along the road.
7. Joe and Jerry are flying kites.
8. Outlaws are stealing all the money.
9. Mike is acting as if his leg was wooden.
10. Kevin is tickling Guy with a feather.
11. The prisoner was begging for some more bread.
12. It is quite obvious that the woman is lying.

15. Using nouns as verbs

Like this:

'Catweazle' is a good *book*. (*book* as a noun)

Did the policeman *book* you for bad driving? (*book* as a verb)

Give me the *answer* at once. (*answer* as a noun)

You must *answer* in ten seconds. (*answer* as a verb)

That group has a fabulous *beat*, man! (*beat* as a noun)

Now *beat* six eggs together. (*beat* as a verb)

1. The officer ordered an immediate attack on the enemy.
2. That laser is sending out a beam of light.
3. Go to the bank and draw some money.
4. Those comedians are a funny act.
5. I like cod fried in batter.
6. That awful bang deafened me.
7. I love to see the cavalry mount a charge.
8. You must not take dogs into the park.
9. Why have you used so much paint?
10. What a peculiar walk James has!

ARE YOU LIKE PRIVATE BONEHEAD?
Try this Munchtest and see!

1. Write down the verbs in these sentences.
a) Joy plays the recorder.
b) Eric fell heavily.
c) James eats in a disgusting manner.

2. Put sensible verbs into the spaces in these sentences.
a) Your neck will not be clean unless you _____ it properly.
b) The dog _____ its dinner quickly.
c) You must all _____ on the rope together.
d) The thunder _____ and the lightning

3. Change these sentences into the past tense.
a) The cook squeezes the lemons.
b) That story bores me stiff.
c) Godfrey buys his shirts in Woolworth's.

4. Change these sentences into the present tense.
a) Richard chose the right box every time.
b) The kind woman gave her fruit to the children.
c) Daniel spoke French and Spanish.

5. Change these sentences into the future tense.
a) I am buying a new bicycle.
b) I bought five stamps.
c) I passed my driving test.

6. Correct the verb in each sentence.
a) Mollie writ me a letter last week.
b) Paul done the whole exercise wrong.
c) English is spoke all over the world.

7. Change the verbs that are written as one word (in *italics*) into similar verbs written with two words.
a) Snowflakes *fall* like white flowers.
b) Mr. Beak *speaks* sharply to Wilfred.
c) Sally *sleeps* soundly.

8. Write sentences using these participles as adjectives.
a) running   b) injured   c) fried   d) galloping

9. Write sentences containing nouns made from these verbs.
a) jump   b) crush   c) run   d) roar

10. Use the nouns (in *italics*) in these sentences as verbs in new sentences.
a) That is a *duck* and not a pheasant.
b) The soldier had a week's *leave*.
c) Tim had a huge *smile* on his face.
d) I cannot stand this awful *place* any more.